EVALUATION

A Team Effort

LINDA PIERCE PICCIOTTO

Scholastic Canada Ltd.

Scholastic Canada Ltd.
123 Newkirk Road, Richmond Hill, Ontario, Canada L4C 3G5

Scholastic Inc.
730 Broadway, New York, NY 10003, USA

Ashton Scholastic Limited
Private Bag 1, Penrose, Auckland, New Zealand

Ashton Scholastic Pty Limited
PO Box 579, Gosford, NSW 2250, Australia

Scholastic Publications Ltd.
Villiers House, Clarendon Avenue, Leamington Spa, Warwickshire CV32 5PR, UK

Design by Yüksel Hassan

6 5 4 3 2   Printed in Canada   2 3 4 5 6/9

Canadian Cataloguing in Publication Data

Picciotto, Linda Pierce
  Evaluation: a team effort

Includes bibliographical references.
ISBN 0-590-73091-6

1. Language arts (Primary). 2. English language — Study and teaching (Primary). I. Title.

LB1528.P53 1992   372.6'044   C92-093243-6

*I would like to dedicate this book to my parents,
Ellen V. and Howard W. Pierce,*

*and to thank the students, staff and parents at South Park School
for all they have taught me.*

CONTENTS

FOREWORD

Linda Picciotto is one of the best teachers I have ever met: her work in the area of curriculum and instruction is inspiring. She now turns with similar insight to the areas of assessment and evaluation. This book provides a blueprint of action for primary teachers, and all of the materials mentioned in it come from Linda's own classroom — a testimony to both their workability and their appropriateness for evaluating young children's progress. She models accountability in the best sense of the word.

Included in her book are suggestions for involving students and their parents in assessment and evaluation. Furthermore, she includes many of the actual techniques and forms she, her students and their parents have used.

Often educators underestimate what their students can do if they are given opportunities to participate actively in their own education. This book demonstrates that the same can be said about evaluation. It clearly demonstrates that children and their parents can participate actively and productively as partners in the evaluation process. Teachers everywhere will find *Evaluation: A Team Effort* not only inspirational but also practical and useful.

Norma Mickelson,
University of Victoria

INTRODUCTION

I teach at South Park School in Victoria, British Columbia, and I count myself fortunate. It's a school where risk-taking and innovation are valued. Parents, administrators and fellow teachers are supportive of "whole language" ideas.

I've been teaching for 14 years and, like most teachers, I've changed over the years. When I began I taught reading by means of readers, but the truth is that I've always found readers boring. I found it difficult to be enthusiastic when presenting an uninteresting story I had already read 20 times, especially one that was written in stilted vocabulary-controlled language. I hated seeing students unhappy because they were still in the Red Book when their friends progressed to Yellow. I can't believe that we even had parent conferences about this problem!

I also hated the standardized tests that told us nothing we didn't already know and that upset the children, making them feel tense and frustrated. I hated marking workbooks in which students were mostly just underlining and circling answers, sometimes at random. They never even looked at the mistakes I had marked; they just looked at their scores. I found the same thing true for math.

Phonics workbooks were worse. They expected the children to learn things even I didn't know, and that no one needs to know to be a reader. I had no idea what an "r-controlled vowel" was; I hadn't been taught to read that way. The children could finish the rest of a workbook page once they'd discovered the pattern for it, but it was obvious that they couldn't use the information in their own work.

I hated having to bribe or bully children to "stay on task" when often the task was frustrating or meaningless to them. But I didn't know what else to do. I began to move away from the readers for longer and longer periods of time so we could do special projects, but I always felt guilty, worried that we were falling behind. Then I did some reading and took a summer course that made me realize that the "special projects" were themselves teaching the skills. So I cheerfully dumped the readers and workbooks and never looked back.

Sometimes I wonder if my students are learning enough, or if they may be missing something they should be exposed to. I wonder whether I'm meeting all their individual needs. That's one reason why I've written this book: it's been a way for me to take stock, to analyze what I'm doing, to see what my students are learning and what I'm learning about them.

Evaluation in Transition

But there's another reason as well: the confusion that exists at the moment about assessment and evaluation. Everywhere new currents in education are suggesting that we teachers need to look for new ways to evaluate our work, our programs, our own performance, the work of our students. We need new techniques that will help us collect the right kinds of data in all areas of the curriculum. We need to collect that data efficiently. We also need to be sure that the information we gather provides valid ways of looking at our students. Authentic, well-organized information helps us know our students better, plan our programs effectively, and write clear anecdotal report cards for parents.

No two teachers use the exact same methods for collecting data because we all have different needs and work in different ways. But we can learn from each other. We all need to discover what works most efficiently in our own classrooms. A checklist or technique useful to one teacher won't necessarily work well for another, but hearing about things that have worked for someone else gives us other options.

This book doesn't describe "the perfect system." Every year I experiment with new ideas, because every year I gain new insights. What works with this year's children may not work at all with next year's group. And as I gain experience I also learn to simplify my procedures, take more pertinent notes and write more clearly and easily.

All I can say is that the techniques in this book have worked or do work well for me. Data collection has become part of my normal daily routine. It allows me to use the knowledge and opinions of my students and their parents together with my own observations when I plan my program and write my reports.

Overview

The book is divided into five parts:

- First I describe how I assess my students, using a variety of open-ended forms I've developed over the years to help me keep my notes in order.

- Next I describe how my students participate in their own assessment and support one another, mostly in informal ways in group or individual discussions. Since I believe it's important to give students a chance to participate actively in their own learning, evaluation and planning, I've developed several forms that provide me with additional interesting information. The kids love to fill them out.

- The part parents play is outlined in the third section. No one doubts any longer that students benefit significantly when school and home maintain good two-way communication and act as partners in the education of the children. I've found that forms are helpful in fostering communication with parents as well.

- The fourth section deals with the actual writing of report cards. I explain how I organize the observations, reports and other material I've gathered, and how I write what I hope are good anecdotal reports. I've included samples written in different styles and for students at different developmental levels.

- In the fifth section I include copies of the forms I use, which you may photocopy for your own classroom use.

EVALUATION BY TEACHERS

Parents and administrators expect — and we want to write — helpful, encouraging, complete reports that provide accurate pictures of how our students are working in all areas of the curriculum, and how they are developing socially. We want to be positive, but we also want to be accurate. We want to assure parents that we really know and care about their children. It's a big task and it's time consuming, but it's important.

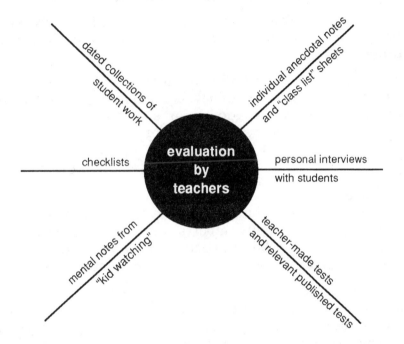

Observations

Most teachers I know agree that the best way to come to know students is through observation. We need to organize our programs so we'll have many opportunities to observe our students and note their strengths, their progress, their social interactions and their learning styles. Then we need to use these observations to plan and modify our programs to meet their needs. And our observation notes help us write good anecdotal reports.

We learned little about our students in the past when we asked them to copy words from the board — except how well they could print, how accurately they could copy, how still they could sit, how quickly they could work, and how willing they were to do activities that might be meaningless for them. When they colored in the lines on some worksheet or put together a teacher-made craft project, we discovered only how well they followed our directions, how carefully they worked, and how well they worked with others. What we didn't see is how creative they were, how much artistic sense they had, and how well they could develop their own ideas.

Now we encourage children to follow their own interests, write in their own way and draw their own pictures. We invite their help in making decisions. We can see more clearly exactly where each one is, both developmentally and academically, in many areas.

When we allow children to choose their own activities, we can observe their interactions with others, take note of their interests, observe how they use material, how they care for equipment, and how well they concentrate on their chosen tasks. We note whether they prefer to work independently or if they choose to work and play with others. When children are actively engaged in activities they've selected themselves, discipline tends not to be a problem. We are free to observe, reflect, take notes and interact with individuals.

When we ask students to work in groups, we observe group dynamics and make observations concerning their social development, work habits, leadership qualities and thinking skills.

When we plan activities and assignments in such a way that all students experience success at their own level of development, we help ourselves as well as them. They grow in self-confidence, and we can assess very accurately what each child can do as we come to know them better than we ever could before.

Notes

We make thousands of observations every day. Most of them are mental notes, but some of them have to make their way onto paper — no one can remember everything! It's surprising how many important events or breakthroughs we forget. It's difficult to remember how particular students used to behave or what they used to be able to do, unless we've kept some kind of record.

The question is, what notes should we take? And once we have them, how can we organize and use them? The answer depends a lot on how clear we are about the goals we have for our students' emotional, social, physical, aesthetic and intellectual development. Only when we're clear enough about those can we develop fitting programs and observe appropriately — and decide what notes to take. Periodically I ask myself if a particular goal I have is being met in my classroom, and I focus my notes specifically on that area for a time.

The notes we take should help us remember what each child *can do,* and where he or she is as a learner in all areas. Then we can use them, along with other information we've gathered, to help us write effective report cards.

Data Booklets

In the week or two before I write report cards, I find it useful to collect information in a more systematic way, especially if I feel that for some reason I haven't been able to record as much as I would have liked to in my more random observation notes. Some skills are more difficult than others to assess by just watching. I also find it helpful to have a lot of information about individuals in one place, both for writing reports and for reference during parent conferences.

At this time I prepare a booklet for each student. I design and photocopy pages that have appropriate questions and spaces to collect the information I want. Since I prepare the booklets myself, all the information is relevant to the students in my class and to the goals I've concentrated on during that term. I don't use these like standardized tests; I'm *not comparing* children, but rather finding out more about each child.

In these booklets I often include a questionnaire for completion during individual student-teacher interviews, with space for me to make comments about what the children were thinking (I ask!) and what words they used when they answered the questions or solved the problems. These are the kinds of questions I use with my early primary children:

- When is your birthday?
- What is your telephone number?
- How old are your brothers and sisters?
- Do you know the months of the year?
- Please read these lower case (upper case) letters for me.
- Can you count by 5s for me? By 10s?
- What does the 2 in 23 mean?
- Which is more, 4 or 7? How many more?
- What number comes right before 50?
- I have eight blocks. Shut your eyes while I put some under the cup. Okay, there are three on the table. How many are under the cup?

If you can arrange for a substitute to teach while you conference with the children, you can work efficiently and give each child your complete attention.

If I feel that the children in my class won't be upset by a test-like situation, I might plan to gather some information from all of them at once, during short periods over several days. If some will be upset because they can't keep up or can't do what their neighbors seem to be doing easily, it's better to gather information in a different way. It may be that group assessment gathering is more appropriate for older children.

I might ask the members of the group to provide a sample of their best printing, or to print a dictated sentence — "I love learning to read and write," for example. Another page might consist of story problems similar to those we've solved together in class. After I read each one, the students draw pictures to show their understanding, and then they write the number answer or the appropriate equation. On another page I might ask them to write dictated numbers.

Even though I'm always collecting samples of their writing, I still may ask the students for a sample of their "very best work" to include in this booklet, preferably one with an illustration. They can then evaluate their own work on a "writing self-evaluation" form (see page 53), and that too can be stapled into the booklet.

Since I like to have a visual record of each student's oral reading on a particular day as well, I insert an oral reading record sheet on which I've printed several sentences taken from recent "news" items we've written and read together. A variety of books of different levels of difficulty are also at hand, the easier ones with illustrations and patterned writing. I give the children a choice about what they'd like to read. As they read the sentences or book pages I mark a copy of the text, using whatever symbols I've decided on, and put the marked-up copy into the booklet. I don't worry about counting the number of mistakes. I just want to have a record I can refer to later when I'm analyzing progress, talking to parents or writing the report card. I also make a note of the comments the student makes, his or her attitude toward reading, use of finger-pointing, use of phonics, picture clues, patterns and "logical guesses."

Oral Reading Record

Student name __Sheila__ Date __January__

Legend: ✓ word read by student
| pause
<u>underline</u> word or phrase repeated
Ⓣ word told to student
s/o student sounded-out word
s/c student self-corrected after misreading
substitution: word read is written above

Observations:
✓ knows where to start
✓ left to right movement
✓ return sweep to left
✓ can find words when asked
(__Street__ , __kitten__)
✓ knows what a word is (How many words are there in the first line?)
___ knows what a sentence is (How many sentences are there in this paragraph?)
(said "4" ~ counted lines)

<u>Katie</u> and | her mom found a lost kitten
on Cook Street. She is black and/white better "my cat is better"
She | was | hungry. <u>They will</u> keep her if call? Ⓣ "he or she"
on s/c Ⓣ
no/one calls the S.P.C.A. to claim her

finger pointed
tired at the end.
<u>Re</u> read with only
a little help.

I used to use a tape recorder for this oral reading record, but I found it inefficient. Listening to the tape later was very time consuming, and background noise always seemed to be a problem. I've also tried having parents do the recording, but I found it more helpful to observe the reading myself.

This example shows one student's reading. The marks I use are similar to the ones used by Goodman and Burke as part of their miscue analysis system (see reference, page 36).

On another sheet in the booklet I write out questions I want to ask the children concerning their progress in certain academic or social areas, their favorite times of day, their favorite field trips, their favorite friends — or anything else I think will help me come to know each one better. The students love to give me their opinions. I write down exactly what they say, when possible. Those quotations make wonderful additions to their report cards.

Here are some questions I've used for an end-of-year interview:

- In what area do you think you made the most progress this year?
- What time of day do you like best?
- Which friend do you like to work with best?
- What do you usually do at recess time?
- On which project day did you make the most interesting thing?
- Our playhouse has been turned into a pet shop, a hospital, a castle, a library, a house, and a science lab. Which did you enjoy the most? What did you enjoy about it?

- What do you wish you had done more of this year?
- What made you the happiest? The proudest?
- What are your hopes for next year?

These examples of data booklet pages give an idea of their usefulness:

Let me/spot you with red.
Let me spot you with black.
On your/tail, on your/head.
On your ears, on your back.

How
Now you are/spotted.
You can sail through the sky.
No/worry at all
because spots make you fly.
Goodbye.''

Interview questions   name _Ellen_   date _Fall '91_

1. What is your favourite time of day in the classroom?
   Activity time ("everybody likes that"), reading time; math on the carpet

2. How about music lessons, library time, gym time, recess?
   "Loves" music, library OK, loves gym (Salmon + Trout favou...
   recess OK sometimes

3. Remember our Project Days? (after art... Goldstream trips) Which did you enjoy mo... create? Goldstream — made stuffed fi... in a painted river

4. What was your favourite field trip? pumpkin patch, Goldstream)
   Pump. patch — liked picking own p...

5. What do you usually do during Activit...
   draw, playhouse — usually wi...

6. If I asked you to build a castle wit... two friends, whom would you choose? Why...
   Janet — best friend — has good id...

7. What do you usually do at recess?
   play house under the big tree, s...

8. In what have you made the most progr... far? Writing — use more real sounds
   Reading — read at home now, too

9. Is there something you would like to...
   bears, penguins

10. What is your buddy's name? Do you e... What activity have you enjoyed most?
    Alex — loves...

Fall 1991
Student: Ellen

Interview
What is your full name   Ellen Howard
              age   6
              birthday   Feb. 16
              address   _?_ Yale Aven...
              phone number   386-42...

☑ count to 20
☑ count backwards from 10   slowly — ...
☑ count by 10's   after I started her off...
☐ count by 5's   not yet
☑ read numerals   8 4 6
☐ identify shapes

☐ read double-digit numbers
              12 18

☐ what does the 2 in the...

Circle letters not known by student

b k e f h n
j p a d g m
w u y r v z g a

D G B H R Q   knows — spot checked
C Z I X F A
L R K E M J
P V N S O Q
U Y W T

Writing Workshop

This is my best printing.
This is my best   printing.

Please print the numerals:
0   1   2   3
5   6   5   8

(dictated sentence)
I Like to Red and Rit

Dictated numbers (print the numerals)
1. eight 8   2. thirteen 13   3. eighty-six 86
4. sixty-eight 68   5. two hundred seventeen 207
6. one hundred four 1004   7. one thousand eighteen 100...

Problem Solving
1. How many millions do you...
2. Two birds on in a tree. Three more birds join them. How many are there now in the tree?   3 + 3 = 5
3. Four pigs were eating. Two went away but four other pigs come to eat. How many pigs are eating now?   4 - 2 + 4 = 8
4. You have ten donuts. You can eat two each day. How many days will your donuts last?   5

My brithday is ni 10!Mor day. I will git f...
I will git Sam pasnts   I Kot wbt ni t...

Student Files and Portfolios

The most important source of information for assessment is the dated writing I collect from my students systematically throughout the year. They date and file the writing workshop papers they produce daily, and once a week they draw and write in a folder or binder filled with blank or lined paper. By leafing through this booklet, both the parents and I can see their progress. The booklets completed by students I've taught over several years are particularly interesting!

Examples of student work in art, math, science and other subjects can also be dated and collected in different folders or envelopes.

Recently I set up a system of *portfolios* in my classroom, and this I've found to be very successful. The children all have personal portfolios, the size of a legal folder, in which they place samples of work that demonstrate some "breakthrough," a special interest or ability, something done especially carefully, or something they found particularly clever or funny — whatever the students (or I, or their parents, or another teacher) found important and noteworthy.

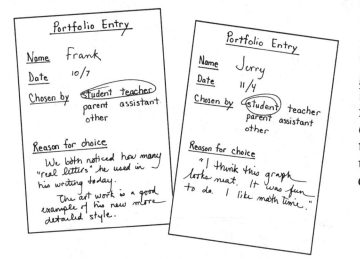

Special small forms are ready to be glued or taped to the back of each work selected, giving the name and date and a brief explanation of the reason for inclusion. Older students can put down their reasons themselves; another adult or I usually scribe for the younger ones. For example:

- I wrote a lot today, and I used a lot of lower case letters.
- It was really hard for me to draw that guy sitting down like that, and I like the way it turned out.
- That is the biggest number I've ever written. It's a centillion.

For times when nothing concrete is produced or when work too large for the folder I designed a "special accomplishment" form. Entries may include notes about a large or three-dimensional work of art, new musical skills, a new physical ability, a discovery or new interest in science or social studies, or even a new personal skill. For example:

- I can skip now.
- I worked well with my group when we painted our mural. It turned out great.
- I performed a great science experiment for the class. It worked really well, and they liked it.
- I can count by 2s and 10s.
- I helped Janet join in. She was happy.

8

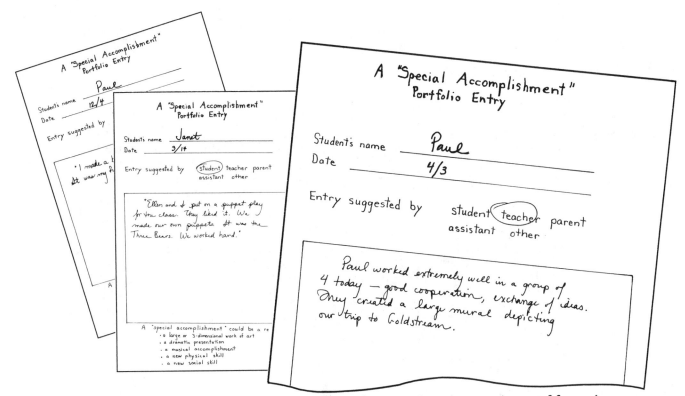

Each entry provides evidence of how that student is growing and learning both in and outside of school. I don't compare children: each is developing at his or her own rate. Students with disabilities can use the portfolios in the same way the other members of the class do. By asking the students to compile their own portfolios I'm asking them to become aware of their own progress and increasingly responsible for their own learning. Also, the portfolios prove very useful when I write report cards and have conferences with parents.

Checklists

Sometimes published checklists are helpful. Some teachers may even use them as the authors intended! They can provide guidance about what to look for in different curriculum areas; they can help new teachers learn more about child development; they can be helpful in suggesting vocabulary for report writing and parent conferences.

Checklists are often included in the guidebooks that accompany math and reading textbooks, or in other types of professional books. This sample is one of several found in *The Learners' Way* by Anne Forester and Margaret Reinhard.

Student Cards

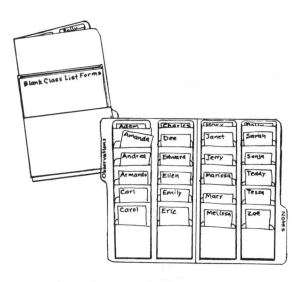

A legal-size filing folder with library card pockets makes a good container for notes about individual students. The pockets are simply overlapped and glued on. I write the names of my students on small cards and slip them into the pockets in alphabetical order. Since the container folds, it's relatively private and easy to store and use. I keep blank copies of the class list forms in a large pocket on the back of the folder as well, where they're easy to find.

My comments on these small cards generally concern the students' behavior, special interests or abilities I notice during the day, and incidents or dialogues I want to remember. I write the date on the card whenever I make an entry. Of course I take more notes about my "special needs" students than about others. But having a card ready for every student reminds me that I need to look at everyone, including the quiet, compliant children who may be overshadowed by their more assertive peers.

FRANK

9/13 — shy, seems nervous, asked me about Mom— when will she pick me up
— in gym, watched only

9/15 — interested in computer. Played "Face Maker" with Carl. Learned quickly

10/3 — a little less nervous. Willing to try "pretend writing" after modeling and encouragement. OK when Mom was late (until he saw her!)

10/10 — active in floor hockey! noisy in activity time — played w/cowboy set w/Jerry

10/17 — very kind to Sarah — shared encouraged at math time

SHEILA

1/29 — helped others in group solving math problem

often chooses 3-d building in act. time, alone or w/others.

2/7 saw many patterns when we looked at our graph of temperatures last month

2/9 supportive of others during Author's Circle

2/15 was more assertive about her own wants during group project time

2/20 told me she loves art — "wants to be an artist"

PAUL

9/10 — trouble sitting still at "carpet time" — distracted, fiddled

9/12 conflicts w/ friends left him feeling sad, angry — asked to "be left alone"
loves to be 1st in line

9/15 frequent conflicts in gym — had him sit out 3 times — diff. for him to admit he was "caught" — argued, quit game

9/18 showed self-control when he was tripped accidentally — sent home note

9/20 better on carpet if he sits at my feet

I also record observations other professionals make to me about my students, so that all the information I have will be in one place. For instance, I might record comments from the learning assistant teacher, the music teacher, the counselor, the nurse, the speech therapist, substitute teachers, other teachers, classroom assistants, parents — or even from the secretary, the custodian and the lunch monitors. All these people provide me with important information at times.

Additional Forms

I've developed some additional forms to help me organize the notes I want to take and the information I need to collect.

Class List Forms

I use class list or "class sweep" forms to make notes when I'm observing more than one student participating in a particular activity. By using forms that include the names of all the members of the class I'm sure that I'm observing all students, and not merely those who stand out in one way or another.

I've found it convenient to have several forms with varying amounts of space for different occasions. You may find you can photocopy some of my forms as they are, adding the names of your own students as you make your notes. Or you may want to make a single copy, write in the names of your students (in alphabetical order by first name), and then make as many copies as you want to have on hand. It's a good idea to use a different color of paper for each different form you copy.

Use a three-hole punch after you photocopy the forms so they'll be ready to put into a binder when you've filled them in. Or you might store them on clipboards or in labeled folders. The completed forms can be organized chronologically or by subject.

Single-side class list:

I use this form (see page 38) when I don't need a lot of space for comments and when I want to see all of the students' names on one side of the paper. I use it to keep track of what the students do during activity time or on project days, for example, or of which books each student selects during reading time. I take a copy of the form on a clipboard to the gym, to the library, or outside when I'm on duty, so I can take notes in different settings.

Since there isn't much room to write, I've found codes useful. For example, *C* means *cooperative play*, *A* means *associative play* and *S* means *solitary play* when I take notes during activity time. I often record which children are working or playing together.

Double-side class list:

I use this form (see page 39) when I need more room to write. For instance, I make more elaborate notes about reading progress as I listen to the students reading the daily news, or a book of their choice. Or I record how they work while participating in a math activity, or how they respond during a conference. By photocopying on both sides of a sheet, I can put all members of the class on one sheet of paper.

Group Form

Often students work in groups, either on their own initiative or in response to my request. This gives me opportunities to note how individuals work together and what skills each one is developing. I use this form (see page 40) to record my observations and write down interesting dialogues. Since group members will change from day to day, I keep blank copies of the form on hand and fill in the names while the groups are working.

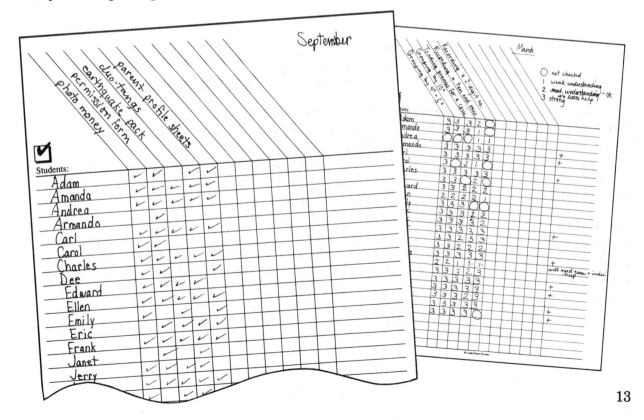

Subject: Castle building w/art box material **Date:** Feb 16.

Students in Groups:

Sheila Jerry Carol	Good cooperation, all participated in planning + choosing materials — good support of each other (J) creative idea for drawbridge — worked w/good concentration and skill (S) figured out how to attach towers to walls, got (C) to help (C) "the gardener" — made little plants to go around the castle
Paul Frank Armando	(P+F) planned together, cooperated, helped each other, tried to include (A) but came to me to complain. (A) really wanted to do his own — A told him this was a group project. Finally decided to "do what the others were doing." w/his help they finished and did a nice job of presenting their work. A breakthrough for Armando!
Janet	Made a very large castle on the floor using stiff paper + lots of tape. Painted it all in bright colours — very happy across, all involved. added flowers

(behind, partially visible left sheet:)

Subject: Math —
Students in Groups:

Jerry
Sheila
Frank

Paul
Dee
Melissa
Ed

Amanda
Andrea
Teddy
Eric

Carl
Sarah
Charles
Ellen

Polly
Emily
Mary
Armando

Class Checklist

I use a simple checklist (see page 41) for the many "housekeeping" chores I have to do — like listing who has turned in notices, money or assignments. I also find this format useful when checking to see which concepts the students have mastered. Other teachers have developed elaborate systems using specific symbols (perhaps also color coded) for "at a glance" recording.

September checklist

Columns: photo money, permission form, earthquake pack, duo-tangs, parent profile sheets

Students:

Adam
Amanda
Andrea
Armando
Carl
Carol
Charles
Dee
Edward
Ellen
Emily
Eric
Frank
Janet
Jerry

March checklist

0 not checked
1 weak understanding
2 mod. understanding — ok.
3 strong

EVALUATION BY STUDENTS

It's crucial that we involve our students in the assessment and evaluation of their own work, and that we allow them to express their opinions about school programs. When we include them in the appraisal and planning processes, we're telling them that they are important and that what they think matters to us. We are helping them become increasingly responsible for their own learning.

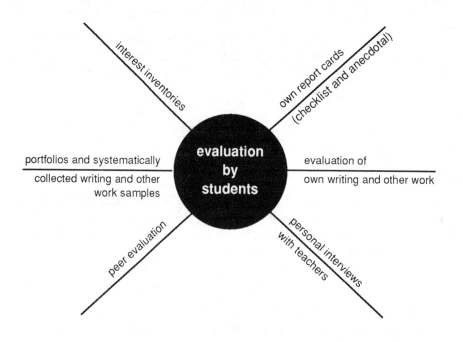

There are many opportunities each day to give our students a chance to make choices:

- Which book shall we read?
- Which game shall we play? Let's vote.
- It's Mary's turn to choose.
- Which piece of work do you want to include in your portfolio?

We can also give them opportunities to evaluate and solve problems:

- I didn't think that tag game went very well. What could we do to make it work better next time?
- How should we arrange ourselves on the carpet so everyone can see Lauren's science experiment?

It's easier to build a wonderful learning environment and a warm community feeling when we ask the children to contribute in meaningful ways.

Peer Evaluation

I can think of no more rewarding or enjoyable times than when we meet as a group to discuss work that's in process or that has been completed. A child reads a report, shares a story or shows a painting. A group of children discusses a construction project, shows a mural or displays a beautiful "pattern block" design. Then the class discusses the merits of the work, offering suggestions to the authors, the architects, the artists. Comments are positive and questions thoughtful. The students enjoy showing and talking about their work because they know that their peers will acknowledge their progress, and that suggestions will be helpful rather than hurtful.

But before all this can happen, I have to spend a lot of time modeling how to make constructive comments. When necessary, I remind individual students about the needs of others. I try very hard not to set up competitive situations.

During Author's Circle time, we sit on the carpet to listen to students read and show their daily writing workshop work. The comments we make to each author will depend on his or her developmental stage. We don't consider one author "better" than another, but we do acknowledge that we're all in different stages of development. Here are some sample comments:

Ellen: "Wow, Janet, that's a neat volcano. What are those two smaller hills?"

Jerry: "You started your sentence with an upper case letter."

Paul: "That's a really interesting story about the cougar, Emily. Did you really see the chase, or did you see it on TV?"

Polly: "I liked the action words you used. I think most of your words are written in standard spelling, aren't they? Your printing is neater today."

Frank: "That's a really great castle, Eric. It must have taken you a long time to draw. What will happen to the knight who's riding his horse on the drawbridge? Are you going to add to the story tomorrow?"

Sarah: "Sonja, you are starting to use more lower case letters!"

If your class is large you could form smaller groups, once your students are familiar with the routines, or you could ask only a certain number to share their writing each day.

The same kind of peer evaluation can take place when students or groups of students show and explain projects they've completed, either on their own or in response to an assignment. It's a time when critical thinking skills and analytical abilities are developed. From a teacher's point of view, it's not only wonderful to see the wide variety of interesting work they've produced, individually or in groups, but it's also gratifying to see how supportive they are of each others' efforts. There's no doubt in my mind that when students know they will be showing and explaining their work to an appreciative audience, they try to produce high-quality, interesting work.

These sharing times provide me with an ideal opportunity to make notes. Usually I don't write until after the sharing, however, since I want to be attentive when someone is speaking. That, too, is good modeling.

Student-Teacher Conferences

During conferences with my students — discussions about writing or reading, individual math evaluations, talks about behavior — I'm careful to:

- ask the students for their opinions;
- encourage them to evaluate their own work or actions;
- question them about their thinking processes;
- ask them to comment on their progress;
- involve them in decision-making and planning.

  I ask questions like these:

- What will you concentrate on in your writing tomorrow?
- What will you try besides kicking the next time you and Charlie have a disagreement?
- What could you do to make solving that type of math problem easier for yourself?

  Sometimes I take notes during or following these conversations, for the purpose of recording patterns and progress.

Self-Evaluation

In addition to these personal conversations, I find it important — and also efficient — to gather *written* data from the students concerning their opinions and their perceptions about their own progress in the different academic and social areas. You may find the following forms useful for this purpose.

My Lilypad Report

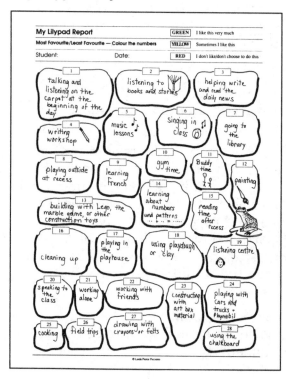

Students love to complete the lilypad form (see page 42). They appreciate the opportunity to tell what things they like to do at school and what things they don't like as much. The skills they have to use just to complete the form are many: keeping their place, thinking about the activity, choosing the correct crayon.

To use this form, first make one photocopy of it. Then fill in each lilypad with an activity you want your students to consider. The students might enjoy helping you decide what to include.

It's a good idea to go through your completed form with a few children in any case. They can tell you if any of the lilypads are unclear, so you can change the wording if necessary. For younger students you might add little drawings on some of the lilypads to make the form more interesting and to help them keep their place when they're using it.

When you've completed your master form, you can run off a class set and give one to each student, along with three pens or crayons: green, yellow and red. After you've read and discussed each item, ask the students to fill in the appropriate box with the color of their choice to indicate whether they like an activity very much (green), so-so (yellow), or not very much (red).

I've discovered that I have to be careful about taking any response too seriously, since some students make their choices for unexpected reasons. Melissa colored LIBRARY red because she sometimes forgets her books. Sarah colored PAINTING red because she paints more at home than at school. Carl doesn't really know why he painted LEGO yellow: it's his favorite activity.

Parents like this report. It's a good basis for conversations not only with you, but also with their child.

My Own Report Card

This form contains a collection of statements that focus on student performance, participation and perceptions in all areas of the curriculum (see pages 43-50). There are eight pages altogether. I make a photocopy of the pages I want to use.

If you want to use these forms, you'll need to look carefully at the questions to decide which items on each page you want to include and what you'd like to add. If you don't have a "buddy time," for instance, you'll want to delete that section. If your students are older, you may want to add something about learning cursive writing, or a more specific math, science, or P.E. topic.

After I prepare my master copies I photocopy the pages on two sides of the paper and make a booklet for each child. The students draw the appropriate symbols next to the items as I explain them. Older students might want to complete the forms using words instead of symbols.

Sometimes I send the blank booklets home for the children to complete with a parent. Parents enjoy the chance to discuss their children's feelings about their schooling, and it's interesting to consider the results when I examine the forms later, perhaps during the parent-teacher interview.

Through the kinds of items it includes, this form signals to the children what is valued by our school and our community, while giving me insights into the students' opinions and feedback about my program.

Karen Abel, a teacher of eight- and nine-year-olds, chose to rewrite the form to give it a more mature look for her older students, and to add some of her own categories. She says that parents are particularly interested in their children's responses on the last two pages, where they indicate the areas in which they've made the most progress and the things they'd like to be able to do better.

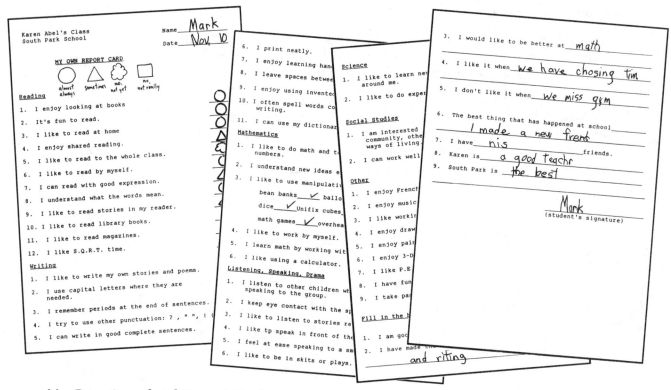

My Own Anecdotal Report Card

My teaching associate Margaret Reinhard has used this open-ended anecdotal format successfully for years.

I ask my students to complete this report card (see pages 51-52) in their own words, using their own spelling. What can they say about their own work? How do they feel about each area? The results are always interesting, and the report cards are often charming.

My Own Anecdotal Report Card — Student: Ted, Date: Feb.

Reading
Im Begnin to Read loog Books and almos evre noet Im Reading a Book to My mom evre noet we chang I Love Reading

Writing
Im comen alog weth Writing I Love Writing Im god at writing Somtoems I ned hlp wth my wrds

Arithmetic
Im god at Arithmetic somtims its hrd.

My Own Anecdotal Report Card — Student: Sheila, Date: Feb.

Reading
I am lrning to read. Lrning to read is heard for me. I am reading a book that is caed The Cat In The Hat I Love READING!

Writing
I am lrning to write. but I am lrning fast. Writing is fun. I LOVE WRITING!

Arithmetic
I liek arithmetic. I liek doing it.

Here are some more sample comments gathered from different report cards written by six-year-old students.

Writing:

"I'm comen alog weth Writing I Love Writing Im god at writing somtoems I ned hlp wth my wrds"

"I am lrning to write. but I am lrning fast. writing is fun. I LOfE WRITING!"

"My writing is mostley strerd. I can spell Lots of worDS. I Don't froget to arase or cross out Mactakes! My parents and My techer tot me this."

"I rilly Lick Too rite I omost rite all the time"

"Writing is won of my Favrit actevades"

Math:

"I love Math I lieK it gost the same as Writing"

"I LOVE LOVE LOVE Math."

"I am gooD at aDDing op. I can slove lots of Math proplems. I sove Math problems in Lots of Ways."

P.E.:

"I loik P.E. alot and alot and alot. I liek palying weth the perashut."

Music:

"I am a gooD Musishion! I Like to sing. Whan the music techer tells me to sing I Do. I play the pano when I get up."

Favorite activities:

"computr Art and a hol Bonch of othr stof"

Behavior:

"I Be a sweet grill in class and at home. I Be Nice to grills and Boys at Reass anD outsiDe."

"I Doo Prity goD Behavyre most of the tims it Leste I hope I Doo"

"I am god."

Writing Self-Evaluation

I use this form (see page 53) for any piece of writing. The students read their own or a partner's work and then evaluate it according to the categories listed. If you want to ask your students to consider different or more specific aspects of a particular piece, add those things to the form before photocopying it.

My Teacher's Report Card

This open-ended form (see page 54) allows my students to comment on my strengths and suggest improvements. The results are more interesting and valuable if the students aren't limited to answering specific questions. Sometimes the results are surprising!

Recently a group of boys had a wonderful time writing a "fake" report card for me telling me what a terrible job I was doing (see illustration next page). At the end, however, they stated that I was a "wicked dude," which I gather was a compliment.

I've come to the conclusion that younger students don't really understand the concept of teacher evaluation, however. I'd use this form with older students.

My Teacher's Report Card
Date
Student reporter
Teacher's name

FAKE   You are terubl at Getr!
        You are terubl at Reding
        You are terubl at hand Riting

Linda Picciottos
Rreport card!

YOU ARE WEKID DuD

My Teacher's Report Card
Student reporter: Ellen   Date Nov. 5
Teacher's name: Linda

Linda Lotas do Math, Riding
Wrcsap, Licsind to tap,
Reed book. she did Simin Sa2.
I Like her very mach

My Teacher's Report Card   A+   A+
Student reporter: Carol   Date Nov. 5
Teacher's name: Karen   A+

Karen is a great teacher She has
good ideas like beat the teacher
or hide a Word on the morning news.
Karen is a very helpfull teacher
She knows a lot about math.
She is very pachant Karen has a
good sense of humer!! She likes to
Jounz in When David comes in.
She dosn't lathe at your falfts.

Additional Forms

As I mentioned in the preceding section, I gather valuable information from other professionals working in the school or district, as most teachers do. But another ready source of information is sometimes overlooked: older students.

In our school we have a buddy system where older students are matched with young ones for sharing and support. If they're well-prepared for the task, older buddies can be helpful in gathering certain kinds of information. For instance, this is a form I recently used to have older students collect information about how their younger buddies performed a series of simple tasks in the gym.

Parents or teacher assistants can also help in the collection of straightforward information. They can print comments young students make, or transcribe into standard spelling statements they've written. Because they have time to observe the students while you're teaching, their comments can be very valuable.

EVALUATION BY PARENTS

Parents are educators. In the few short years before children enter school, their parents have taught them more than they'll learn throughout their school years, perhaps even for the rest of their lives. And parents don't stop teaching when their children enter school. That's why education has to be seen as a joint effort of the home, the school and the community.

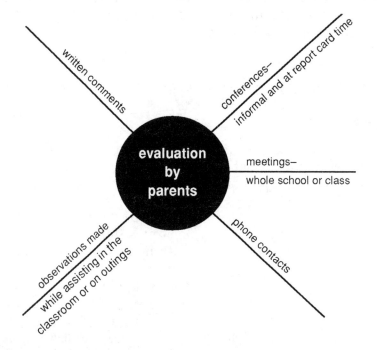

Communication with Parents

The more we learn about our students and their families, the better able we are to prepare appropriate programs to meet the children's needs. We reap tremendous rewards when we welcome parents into the classroom and when we take the time to make occasional telephone calls or write quick notes to keep in touch. The children also benefit when they know that adults who care about them are working together to make their school years the best they can be.

Family Meetings

At our school we've set up regular family meetings. Once every two months the parents of the students in each class meet informally in the home of one of the parents. The teacher attends too. The parents who serve as the "class coordinators" for the year run the meeting, which provides information not only about current events in the school, but also about changes in school programs or policies. The parents are asked for their opinions about issues that are important to the school as a whole, and these are reported back to the school executive at other regularly scheduled meetings. The school executive consists of elected officers, a coordinator from every class, the principal, and a teacher representative.

At the family meetings I have a chance to discuss my plans, request help for certain projects or trips, and ask for ideas. The contributions the parents make enrich my program tremendously, and a strong feeling of community develops because the parents come to know me and each other much better. Some parents welcome the opportunity to discuss educational philosophy or child-rearing concepts with me and the other parents. Good communication usually leads to good understanding, and I always come away from these meetings feeling happy that I have the help, support and confidence of so many people.

Effective report cards are easier to write once I've met and talked with the children's families in these friendly meetings, and parent-teacher conferences become less stressful for all participants.

Parent Observations

My form for observations by parents (see pages 55-56) gives me an easy way to collect *written* information from parents. Most parents appreciate the structure provided by the questions, but some prefer to write a short letter about their child instead. The replies are always interesting, and often very revealing.

You can decide when you'd like the parents to complete the form. You may want to gather information at the beginning of the school year, or you may want to wait until later, perhaps just before writing the first report.

Observations by Parents
Student: Frank   Teacher: Linda

Your child's attitude towards school and/or learning:
- not enthusiastic first thing in the morning, but
- when asked about school he says he likes to
- somewhat unsure about his ability to a
- enjoys being with his friends but is a
  noisy crowds

Your child's behaviour:
- comfortable on the "fringe" of the
- gets very angry when he feels he's
  or cheated
- has high expectations of himsel
- easily frustrated
- considerate towards younger ch

Your child's special needs (environment, rules, learning style...):
- he needs to know exactly what is e
  instruction has to be very clear
- doesn't like to be overly notice
- prefers a low key atmospher
  new to absorb

Your child's physical development:
- very co-ordinated
- good muscle development
- hand-eye co-ordination in

Anything else?
Frank is a very coopera
I'm hoping that as his
spontaniety will bloss

Thank You

© Linda Perez Picciotto

Observations by Parents
Student: Frank   Teacher: Date: Sept.
                                Parent: Diane

Teachers are interested in how you see your child at *home*. Please take a minute to make notes about his or her social and academic development, interests, attitudes, strengths and special needs. When you write, use phrases or brief comments.

Your child's interactions with other children or with siblings: Friends are important to him and he has certain expectations of them. Problems arise when they fall short of these expectations. Although their short-comings are rather mild to me, he takes them quite seriously and we have many conversations about forgiveness, tolerance, understanding, etc. I think he's a little confused about human nature and therefore a little frustrated.

Your child's interests and activities at home:
- enjoys reading books, playing board games, watching movies, playing cards, drawing (we do a lot of that) and making "stuff".
- riding in the skiff.
- going to parks
- soccer + running

Your child's previous or present experiences that you consider significant:
Frank is an only child and has spent a lot of time by himself or in the company of other adults. The three of us spend a lot of time together.

Your child's structured activities outside school (sports, music, art lessons...?):
- "dance + drama" once a week
- Saturday morning soccer
- swimming twice a week
- skating sometimes.

A Negotiated Report

Several interesting ideas concerning reporting have been published recently. In our area, Alison Preece and Terry Johnson have recommended a negotiated report (see *Prime Areas*, Spring, 1990). They suggest that about a month before reporting time teachers send home a letter asking parents to indicate if they'd like focused comments on certain aspects of the curriculum. If they are interested in two or three areas (arithmetic and social development, for example), then the teacher can concentrate on those when collecting data and writing. Of course these wouldn't be the only areas discussed in the report, but they'd be written more thoroughly. Parents surveyed after a trial run of this system reported that they appreciated being consulted about the content of the report card.

When we suggest changes to reporting procedures, however, we have to be careful that what we propose truly facilitates communication. We want to be sure that we aren't simply increasing our workload or confusing parents!

Parent Conferences

One of the best ways to facilitate the kind of communication and cooperation we want to establish with parents is to make good use of regular conferences.

Parent-Teacher Conferences

Student-led conferences have become popular with many teachers at our school, but at times we still arrange for parent-teacher conferences in a more or less traditional way. Parents sign up for 20-minute time slots during a specified afternoon (1:00-5:00) or evening (4:00-9:00). On both of those days the students are dismissed at 12:15 so the teachers won't be working 12 hours on one day. During the evening meetings, a common half-hour break is arranged so the teachers can eat a potluck or catered supper together in the staff room.

I leave samples of the students' work in the hall for parents to examine if they arrive early for their conference. I also put out paper, pens and books for the children who come with their parents, and a "mailbox" so that parents can write notes to their children. The students love to find notes for them the following day. If I've made a videotape or slides of the students at work during their school day, I set up a VCR and/or slide projector for the parents to operate. Parents who can't come into the classroom during school hours appreciate this opportunity to watch their children in the school setting.

For the conference itself I have handy the students' files, portfolios, writing folders, works of art, evidence of math knowledge, books currently being read, special projects, and anything else I want to show. Tea/coffee and cookies are always appreciated as well! Parents usually want to discuss their children's report cards (not only the one from me, but also any the children themselves have written) and to tell me what's happening at home that they think might be affecting their children. I also take the opportunity to tell them how they might help the children at home.

I write down any decisions we make that require action (see page 57). Should a school counselor become involved? Should the parents begin an evening reading program? If you use carbon paper, both you and the parents will have a copy.

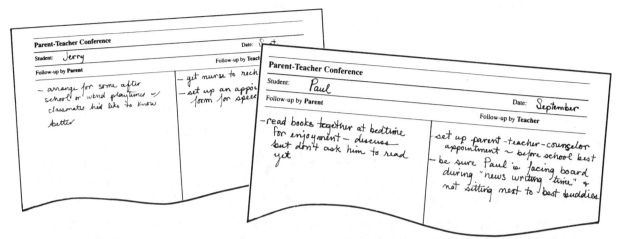

Parent-Teacher Conference Date: _____

Student: _Jerry_

Follow-up by Teacher

Follow-up by Parent

— arrange for some after school or wknd playtimes w/ classmates he'd like to know better

— get nurse to rech___
— set up an appoi___ form for spee___

Parent-Teacher Conference

Student: _Paul_ Date: _September_

Follow-up by Parent

Follow-up by Teacher

— read books together at bedtime for enjoyment — discuss but don't ask him to read yet

— set up parent-teacher-counselor appointment ~ before school best
— be sure Paul is facing board during "news writing time" & not sitting next to best buddies

Some teachers encourage their students to participate in these conferences. They believe that doing so helps the students to feel more involved with their own learning. Issues the parents may want to discuss in private can be taken up at a different time, perhaps by phone. This approach is probably more appropriate for older students, however. When I tried it with young children, I found it awkward. The level of language I had to use so the children would understand wasn't really appropriate for the parents — and I sometimes found myself talking about the children as if they weren't there!

Nevertheless, I like the idea of students conferring with their parents in the classroom setting.

Student-Led Conferences

Margaret Reinhard and I thought that asking our students to explain their progress and plans to their parents would be a good way of involving them in their own learning in a direct way. So we decided to try student-led conferences. We thought that the preparation for and management of these conferences would be excellent personal and educational experiences for the children. After hearing our enthusiastic explanations, the parents agreed.

The students prepared by collecting samples of their work in folders, helping to choose which math and science activities to share with their parents, which parts of favorite books to read or show, which pieces of writing to discuss, which works of art to display, and which gym activities to demonstrate. We created a checklist for the students to follow as they led their parent or parents to each center. On the form were spaces for encouraging comments from the parents.

If you feel the parents might be nervous about these conferences, you could list a few questions they can ask at the different centers. I found that the children took charge and didn't need much adult guidance, but the list could be there just in case. My students "walked through" their plans with me the day before; some teachers suggest that the students practice with their older buddies.

The parents signed up for one of three two-hour time periods. Approximately one-third of the students came to each session with one or two parents. Margaret and I circulated, answered questions and made encouraging comments, but the students were in charge. A short chat between parent, teacher and student was also part of the program.

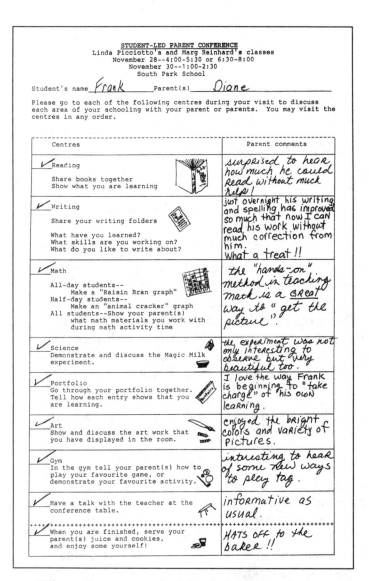

STUDENT-LED PARENT CONFERENCE
Linda Picciotto's and Marg Reinhard's classes
November 28--4:00-5:30 or 6:30-8:00
November 30--1:00-2:30
South Park School

Student's name **Frank**   Parent(s) **Diane**

Please go to each of the following centres during your visit to discuss each area of your schooling with your parent or parents. You may visit the centres in any order.

Centres	Parent comments
✔ Reading Share books together Show what you are learning	surprised to hear how much he could read without much help!
✔ Writing Share your writing folders What have you learned? What skills are you working on? What do you like to write about?	just overnight his writing and spelling has improved so much that now I can read his work without much correction from him. What a treat!!

✔ Math
 	
All-day students--
  Make a "Raisin Bran graph"
Half-day students--
  Make an "animal cracker" graph
All students--Show your parent(s)
  what math materials you work with
  during math activity time
	the "hands-on" method in teaching math is a GREAT way to "get the picture".

✔ Science Demonstrate and discuss the Magic Milk experiment.	the experiment was not only interesting to observe but very beautiful too.
✔ Portfolio Go through your portfolio together. Tell how each entry shows that you are learning.	I love the way Frank is beginning to "take charge" of his own learning.
✔ Art Show and discuss the art work that you have displayed in the room.	enjoyed the bright colors and variety of pictures.
✔ Gym In the gym tell your parent(s) how to play your favourite game, or demonstrate your favourite activity.	interesting to hear of some new ways to play tag.
✔ Have a talk with the teacher at the conference table.	informative as usual.
✔ When you are finished, serve your parent(s) juice and cookies, and enjoy some yourself!	HATS OFF to the baker!!

When they were finished showing their work, the students offered their parents a snack which the class had prepared.

Spending time in the classroom gave the parents a chance to observe the kinds of activities their children enjoyed, and we came to know the students better as we watched them interact with their parents. If a child was a member of two families, because of divorce or other circumstances, we made provision for a second conference on another day.

The parents were impressed by how much their children were learning and by how aware they were of their own progress and needs. The students loved having their parents' undivided attention. The ones who led more than one conference were doubly blessed — they enjoyed the attention of two different sets of adults! Because siblings weren't invited, this was an opportunity for each child to shine. Almost all of the parents who responded to our questionnaire said that they would like the next conference to be student-led as well.

Those parents who felt that they needed a private conference with the teacher were given an appointment for another day, but very few requested the extra meeting. The report cards and the student-led conference had given them all the information they needed.

There are many ways to approach conferences. Perhaps the first one of the year could be a parent-teacher conference and the second one a student-led conference. Not every teacher and not every school will operate in the same way; different schools and different teachers must determine what works best for them. The goal is always to create and maintain good school and home communication.

REPORT CARDS

We want our report cards to be helpful and constructive, not destructive and discouraging. We want them to be personal, positive, encouraging and complete. The purpose is to communicate with the parents to make clear what we as teachers and they as parents can do together to best help the children learn.

Of great importance to most parents is the knowledge that:

- the teacher knows and likes their children;
- their children are happy at school and are "doing OK";
- their children get along well with others and have friends.

Writing an Anecdotal Report

Generally parents aren't looking for long essays. I've been experimenting with a "point form" style (see samples). I like it, and so do the parents. The report card seems clearer to them, they say. And I don't have to spend as much time composing and editing as I did with the paragraph style. Sometimes, however, and for some children, a "letter style" seems more appropriate.

Whatever style we use or length we write, our reports should be personal and detailed enough so it's apparent we really do know the children. It's good to include some bits of conversation we've had with the children, or some revealing comments we've overheard.

Report cards should contain no real surprises. Any problem areas we might mention should have been discussed with the parents beforehand, either in person or by telephone. Saying "As we discussed . . ." when we write lets everyone know we've taken this step.

We need to focus on what the students *can do* rather than what they can't. We want to be sure we're giving the parents a clear picture of their children's development and needs. For instance:

- When we say Alice has become more interested in letters and words in books, and can now read the names of her classmates, her parents know she's at the emergent reading stage. Saying "Alice can't read yet" is unnecessary.

- When we tell Ron's parents we're helping him learn some conflict-resolution techniques, we're also saying Ron has some problems relating to his classmates.

We want to emphasize that education doesn't start and stop at school: it's a joint home/school responsibility. If there's something the parents can do at home to help, they want to hear about it: "Be sure to enjoy books with Alan at home, but at this point it will be better if you don't pressure him to read to you. He will when he feels ready."

Deciding what words and phrases to use in report cards is a challenge. Nothing is gained by being negative. Negative report cards simply leave the children believing that they're bad or stupid or hopeless or inferior — and parents sad, angry, defensive or discouraged! On the other hand, our reports must be realistic and comprehensive. There are many ways of sending the same message; report card writing is a real art.

The following examples show two different reports on a specific observed behavior. The "encouraging" paragraphs are always longer, but many teachers find that a more informal, chatty style doesn't really take much longer to write.

Robin

(Seven-year-old. Developmentally delayed, but seems bright. Not yet reading, but beginning to remember a few sound-symbol correlations. Parents worried.)

Discouraging approach:

Robin is below grade level in her reading. She can't read anything except the word "we" and her own name. Be sure to read to her at home.

Encouraging approach:

Robin is keenly interested in our group writing and reading activities. She follows the line of print with a pointer when she "reads" our daily news or a big book. She paraphrases the message as she remembers it and is pleased when she can recognize words like "we," "and" and "I." This is a beginning! I'm sure we'll see good progress in this area when she's ready, because her attitude is so positive. Robin tells me that reading time after recess is one of her favorite times of the day. Continue to enjoy books together at home.

Lucy

(Six-year-old. Has a short attention span, even during story time. Squirms on the carpet, pokes neighbors, fiddles with toys, sometimes gets up to wander.)

Discouraging approach:

Lucy can't sit still. She rolls around on the carpet and bothers her neighbors. She constantly fiddles with toys and doesn't pay attention to the lessons, or even to stories.

Encouraging approach:

As we discussed in our phone conversation, Lucy has some difficulty sitting in one spot on the carpet for any length of time without distracting her classmates. I'm helping her focus better by asking her to sit next to me. When she's near I can quietly let her know when her actions distract me or her classmates, and I can encourage her to increase her attention span by praising her when she's behaving appropriately. I've already noticed improvement, and Lucy tells me that she now enjoys story time more.

Gerald

(Six-and-a-half-year-old. Has a lot of trouble understanding math concepts. Needs one-to-one help to understand directions and is confused when he attempts to solve problems the group works on together.)

Discouraging approach:

Gerald has a lot of trouble understanding numbers. He can't count backwards and he can't solve story problems without a lot of help. He should memorize number combinations to 10.

Encouraging approach:

Gerald understands numbers to 10 and is able to count by 2s, using his fingers to "count" on. He can write and read some numbers under 100 and he can often answer number questions during calendar time. I plan to work with him on counting backwards starting with numbers greater than 10. He has some trouble with the story problems we work on as a class, but often he can catch on when I help him individually. Working with manipulative materials, playing board and card games, and solving real-life problems as they come up at home will help him. I'll give you more suggestions at our conference.

Susie

(Six-and-a-half-year-old. Not well liked by other students because she tends to be bossy. Often tattles about her classmates and calls out answers in class.)

Discouraging approach:

Susie has trouble making friends because she's bossy. She calls out in class instead of raising her hand. She asks me to help her instead of solving social problems herself.

Encouraging approach:

Susie's wish to be in charge creates social problems for her. I'm working to help her learn a variety of social problem-solving techniques to make her aware of how she relates to classmates and when it's appropriate for her to seek adult help. I'm hoping she can learn to give others a chance to lead in some activities. She's perceptive and contributes a lot to our discussions. She works well independently, with good concentration. During sharing time everyone is eager to see what she has created — she's very creative and her projects are often humorous.

There are resources to help us write report cards:

- We can share our experiences with our colleagues and advise each other.
- Published checklists in different curriculum areas can help with wording and content.
- Curriculum guides, particularly new ones that support our more open-ended, child-centered approaches, are very useful.
- Many published books and articles about evaluation offer suggestions.

Sample Report Cards

Sheila

Before I started to write the following report card, I gathered Sheila's earlier reports and all the information I'd collected about her since the last one. These let me see and comment on the progress she'd made, and helped make sure that I didn't use the same words and points as before. That information included:

- her data booklet (see pages 4-7);

- her portfolio (this included the next three items — see pages 8-9);

- the folder in which she'd been drawing and writing once each week, so I could look at her work and any comments I might have made to myself on the back of the pages;

- her writing workshop file with dated samples of her daily writing;

- any math sheets I might have saved (I rely heavily on my notes for math and other curriculum subjects because I don't usually use worksheets; but I might find a graph, or some other work Sheila completed on her own while solving a problem);

- her card from my individual notes folder (see page 10);

- my binder containing completed class-list sheets, so I could see what I'd written about her in different areas of the curriculum (see pages 11-13);

- any self-evaluation forms she'd completed, both recently and in the past (see pages 16-20);

- any notes her parents had sent to me, and the "observations by parents" form they'd completed (see page 23).

I always make a list of the areas I want to comment on before I begin to write, so my report will flow well from one area to another, and so I won't forget to include any important points. I use a basic list as a guide when I write for all of my students. For Sheila's report (see next page) I jotted down:

- general statement
- social interaction/work habits
- listening/speaking — including author's circle
- writing
- reading
- math
- social studies — hospital, Hannukah
- science — experiments
- activity time
- P.E. — gym and outside
- participation in "Empress's and Emperor's New Clothes"
- closing statement

Then I read through everything that had to do with Sheila, and I wrote. I used a word processor, since it makes editing and proofreading much easier.

Other Samples

The five additional sample report cards (see next two pages) were written for students of different ages and at different stages of development. The first two, like Sheila's, are examples of the traditional paragraph style; the others illustrate the more informal point-form style.

Sheila is making steady progress in her reading and writing. She can read the daily news now without effort. When I read with her I find that she uses different techniques (phonics, context clues, visual memory) to read an increasing number of words. Although reading is not effortless for her at this point, she is well on her way. I noted recently that she was helping one of the younger students read an enlarged book with her. ("You read along with me.") Sheila enjoys books and listening to stories.

She seems to enjoy Writing Workshop, particularly when she has a chance to use the word processor. She usually writes several well-composed sentences, often about things that are happening at school or at home. ("On my birthday we are going to a soe. My sasr is fling a little jls.") She now uses many more letters that are in the words she chooses, both consonants and vowels, but often the ones she leaves out make her writing difficult to read, both for her and for me! In a writing conference I am sure she could tell me that she could have used a "t" in sister, an "sh" in show, and a "e" in feeling, and I'm certain that soon she will be able to include them on her own. Sheila still reverses many letters, but she now has better control when she prints. She has reduced the size of her printing, and her letters are more uniform.

Sheila seems particularly interested in our daily science experiments. Her science notebook is complete and detailed. She describes each experiment accurately and includes charming illustrations.

As I mentioned on the last report, Sheila has a real strength in math. Her good visual skills are evident in her art when she uses math material to create patterns, and when she completes puzzles. When the students were trying to figure out how many candles it would take to complete the Hanukkah Menorah ceremony. Sheila became a group leader: Classmates realized that she knew how to do it, so she soon had several students at her table. Sheila thinks clearly when solving problems.

She is always kind when she works and plays with others, and she is most empathetic. During activity time she often plays with others in the class hospital, plays games, or works on her own on some art project or using math materials. She likes to build towers with the foam blocks.

Sheila likes to go to the gym with the class. She says she likes to play with balls, with the parachute, and she likes games. Recently she joined an active game of floor hockey. Her coordination is good.

She did a great job as the empress in our winter play, "The Emperor's and the Empress's New Clothes."

Jerry *(age 6 years, 10 months)*

As I indicated on the November report card, Jerry is a student with many strengths. He thinks very clearly, he is self-motivated, and he has many interests. He produces high-quality work in all fields. His understanding of mathematics is good. He concentrates well and is a good problem-solver. He enjoys art work and produces interesting things, both on paper and when working on 3-d projects. He has a nice sense of design and color.

His writing is of a very high standard, both in content and in form. His sentences are clear, his spelling and punctuation are almost perfect, and his compositions are imaginative and often amusing. He has written some nice poems this term, and the descriptions of the science experiments he has been writing in his science notebook are accurate and well-written. He is now showing more concern about the neatness of his writing and his work in general, and he has reduced the size of his letters. Jerry willingly shares his writing with the class during Author's Circle. He is now much better able to project his voice, and I find his speech much more understandable.

He makes good contributions to class discussions. He is now almost always "with us" during lessons and talks — I rarely have to ask him to put away a book so that he can participate.

As well as being a strong student, Jerry is a good friend to others and is willing to hel friends when they have difficulty. He works well in a group.

During activity time Jerry's first choice is the computer, but he chooses a variety of activities as well, sometimes on his own and sometimes because the computers are He has enjoyed playing in the class hospital with both all-day and half-day studen He also enjoys playing board gan Recently he has been in puppet-theater groups.

with manipulative material such as Lego and the marble game.

Jerry loves to play in the gym. Recently he enjoyed playing floor hockey. He lik on the new adventure playground.

Jerry did a wonderful job as the Emperor in our production of "The Emperor's and the Empress's New Clothes."

Frank *(half-day student, age: 5 years, 11 months)*

Frank seems to enjoy school, and I am happy to see the growth he is making. He seems to be more self-confident and more relaxed about changes in routine. He plays well with both the half-day students and the older group, and he also works well on his own.

He is always cooperative and he is a good friend to others. He shares well and is considerate.

Activity time is his favorite part of the day. During this time he chooses a variety of tasks. He enjoys working with construction toys and the Playmobil sets, both of which require good small-muscle coordination and good social skills. He has enjoyed using the computer. He learned how to use different programs easily and he is good about teaching others. When he hits a snag, he knows whom to ask for help.

Frank enjoyed being in the play, "The Emperor's and the Empress's New Clothes." I was pleased that he was able to say his line, "But they aren't wearing any clothes!" in front of the large audience.

Frank enjoys singing and going to music lessons.

He enjoys listening to stories and looking at books.

During Writing Workshop Frank is willing to print a few letters to stand for the sentence he writes about his drawings. He is including more details in his art work. When we write the "news" on the board Frank is attentive, but he doesn't volunteer to come up to "read" yet.

Frank is enjoying our daily science experiments. The drawings he completes in his science notebook after each experiment are charming.

In the gym Frank plays happily and actively. He took part in a recent floor hockey game with enthusiasm. His coordination is good. He says his favorite activity is playing with the basketball. Outside, he likes the new adventure playground.

Carol (age: 6 years, 3 months)

OBSERVATIONS AND GROWTH IN GOAL AREAS
— Carol enjoys school: "I like to learn a lot of things every day!"

— always cooperative, responsible, interested

— affectionate, helpful

— empathetic with friends, works well with others and independently

— attends well during "news time" — often volunteers to read the sentences after we have read them together

— knowledge of letter sounds now beginning to appear in her own work: (I ANM WAKEN ASEGARE AND SE SRN: I am walking in the garden and the sun is shining; I LAK TO LRN TO rED: I like to learn to read) At this point she's using upper case letters with occasional spaces between words. She is very pleased that she can use some "real letters." Her writing often includes humor: once she named her cow Heidi because it hides, and during author's circle she asked Mary to play the part of the cow to illustrate her story!

— can read the names of classmates and some familiar words (we, to, mom, from), and enjoys "reading" books with friends that we have read many times together (I Can Fly, Cat and Mouse)

— enjoys listening to taped books at the listening center

— loves to go to the gym — plays actively

— enjoyed astronomy study — says her favorite part was looking in other rooms to see all the projects other students made. Excited about being able to see things in the night sky at home, and wrote about it during writing workshop (the Big Dipper, Mars)

— often chooses art during Activity Time, usually working with or beside Melissa, Emily and/or Mary. Enjoys using felt pens and building with art-center supplies. Sometimes she and her friends make "exactly the same thing."

— art work colorful, full of interesting details

— enjoys music in the classroom and with Marne

— works well during math lessons, understands most concepts

FOCUS FOR NEXT TERM
— continue to enjoy school and work on emerging reading and writing strategies

— continue to work with math manipulatives during lessons and free exploration to strengthen understanding of math

— work on counting and reading numbers higher than 15 and counting by 10s, 5s at home and school

— begin learning to print lower case letters

(age: 6 years, 7 months)

OBSERVATIONS AND GROWTH IN GOAL AREAS
— ...justed very well to all-day program

— ...es well in all activities — cooperative, responsible

— ...during activity time, writing workshop, gym, and music with Marne best. Enjoys the weekly choir.

— ...during discussions, but her comments indicate careful consideration of the topic at hand and ...ful

— ...d concentration independently, often chooses to work on her own when given the choice ...group and is considerate of others, but tends not to be assertive about her own ideas

— ...over at a loss for original ideas for activity time, project days. Recently wrote her own ...pets for "Little Miss Muppet" puppet show (presented to the class)

— ...kshop, Mary is willing to take risks, write words she isn't sure she can spell, so now ...interesting and her subjects more varied. She uses many real or "good guess" letters ...can tell me others she could have included. A recent sentence was: The SPIDER SI ...SPIDERSnaB aND The SPIDERSnaB is baTan The Faws (The spider is going back to ...der web is between the flowers) She seems to really enjoy proofreading her work

— ...read classmates' names, the class news, and many high-frequency words ...to the . . .") Uses a variety of strategies to read familiar books., too (I Can Fly,

— ...ly when solving problems and learning new concepts. Uses good strategies

— ...ecially reading space books and using the "crater-maker"

— ...ly chapter books

— ...and to write long words

— ...in her writing

— ...ng with a partner or small group, sometimes in a leadership role

— ...ctivities to build skills and knowledge in all areas

David (age:...

OBSERVATIC...
— has adjuste...

— gets along...

— interested...

— participates well, work shows involvement ..., asks for clarification if ...

— listens carefully — hears and follows instructions, presently enjoying Wayside Tales from Side...

— enjoys listening to stories — last September he was upset about using... is using "real sounds" in his words! He makes good guesses based on wha... ARABRASRABENMANAEBThPALeSCAMANDrrAStADHAM (A robbe... came and arrested him.)

When we have a conference he can tell me where the spaces should be, ...when he's writing.

— beginning to read — can reread the morning news, classmates' nar... Fly) with just a little help. Concentrates well.

— says he likes music, gym and activity time best

— during activity time he chooses a variety of activities with his fri... computer, Playmobil

— joined the choir that meets Wednesday afternoons — really enj...

— says he has learned more about numbers this year, and that he... concentration during math lessons and activities he chooses him... many problems in his head, too.

— enjoyed astronomy study, says he learned a lot . Especially ... making the lunar landscape, and constructing the rocketship

— loves gym, plays actively, has good coordination

FOCUS FOR NEXT TERM
— begin learning to print and use lower case letters

— start a home reading program. He can choose familiar...

— continue to enjoy school and to experience a wide vari...

Sonja (age: 8 years, 0 months)

OBSERVATIONS AND GROWTH IN GOAL AREAS
— Sonja is now at a point where she is ready to benefit from daily individual attention from our learning assistant teacher. She is enthusiastic about going for her lessons and is very excited about being able to read a little and to use some real letter sounds in her own writing. She works on her writing on her own during other times of the day. She is anxious for her spelling to be RIGHT. I'm hoping that she can be happy when she makes logical GUESSES, for English is so irregular she can't possibly guess RIGHT most of the time! Writing a dictated sentence recently, Sonja wrote "I LKe Len 2 re nat ret" (I like learning to read and write). She can now read the daily news after we have worked on it together first, and she can even read many familiar words at first sight ("Today we are going to go to the . . .")

— learning to solve social problems, but still concerned about ownership and space rights ("She took my paint and I asked first and she didn't even ask me if she could have it.")

— often chooses to work alone

— talks to and often stays with adults (staff members, parents, visitors) likes to converse with adults

— concentrates well on chosen projects and usually during class lessons, though she may be distracted by objects near her

— very observant, perceptive — often comes up with ideas to help solve problems ("We could just use that list you made with us yesterday.")

— good memory for things I've told them, where things were placed

— makes good observations about stories we're reading, notices things in illustrations others may miss (including me!)

— likes to learn about new things, loves to go on field trips

— some math concepts easier for her now, but still finds numbers confusing. Can count by 2s, 5s, 10s, can read numbers below 10.

— likes activity time, usually chooses to "make books and draw"

— enjoyed our astronomy study, especially Betty's visit during which she let us handle a meteorite and showed slides of the solar system. Asked good questions: "If you got near Mercury, would you catch fire or melt?" "How did they take that picture?"

— loves going to gym — plays actively

— plays with Cheryl outside — says she doesn't play with classmates

FOCUS FOR NEXT TERM
— continue to enjoy reading and writing

— provide opportunities for her to work cooperatively in groups

— continue to provide many experiences with math manipulatives

— continue to give opportunities to help solve "real" math problems at home (find "teachable moments")

— continue to enjoy reading together at home, asking her to read herself only when she wants to

Teacher-Parent Reports

The primary teachers at University Hill School in Vancouver have good parent support for the teacher-parent reports they write. These are divided into two sections, one for general observations and a list of the major gains for the term, and one to outline the focus for the next term. At first most of the teachers wrote their reports after the parent-teacher conferences, but in the end they found it more efficient to write their remarks before the meeting, leaving space so the parents could add to either part of the report if they wanted.

They found that this type of anecdotal report, especially if it's written in point form, takes much less time to write than the traditional paragraph-style report, and it supports the idea of parents and teachers working as a team to educate the children. In addition to these personal reports, most teachers write overviews that outline the classroom activities for the term. The samples below were written using a modification of the University Hill School form.

Date February

TEACHER-PARENT REPORT

regarding the progress of

Sheila Steiner

Age: 6 years 11 mont

Observations and growth in goal areas

— beginning to be able to use phonics context
reading familiar and even some new materials
to use picture clues. Helped younger studen
— enjoys stories and books
— using many more "real letters" in her writ
— strength in mathematics very evident. Ha
— empathetic with friends
— can work well both cooperatively and i
— good coordination in gym — participates
— loved being on stage as the Empress in

{ — proud of accomplishments. She says she "a
Reads all road signs and ads!
— Very happy to go to school, seems more relaxe

Focus for next term
— continued writing experience — more w
help her included more letters in her
— provide math enrichment
— work on more uniform printing
— stress reading for pleasure at home

teacher   pare

Date February

TEACHER-PARENT REPORT

regarding the progress of

Frank Fielder

Age: 6 years 0 months

Observations and growth in goal areas

— marked growth in self-confidence. No longer as worried
about changes in routines
— participates more in class discussions
— cooperative, responsible
— good friend — shares and plays well with friends in
both age groups
— makes good use of activity time — uses a variety of centres
— thinks clearly when using the computer & solving problems
with the class
— enjoys singing and now goes happily to music lessons
— willing to print a few letters to stand for his sentence
in writing workshop
— loves books and stories
— art work detailed — drawings are wonderful!
{ — Frank has really "grown up" this term. Excited about school - lots of friends.
— He loves to read with us at home. He pretends to read books himself, using
the pictures as guides. — Interest in science sparked by your science experiments.

Focus for next term
— encourage more participation in discussions
him to "take risks" when he

In the end, each teacher has to decide what works best for him or her. We all work in different settings, with students, parents and administrators who have different needs. We all have to discover by experimenting for ourselves what data-collecting and report-writing techniques are most useful and efficient for our particular circumstances.

Sending the Report Card Home

In the past, report card day was often a worry not only for the students, but also for their parents. The report card was a mystery. It was given to the student in a sealed envelope, to be opened only by a parent or a guardian. Usually the children had little idea about what to expect — so they expected the worst!

At our school we've found a way to take the mystery and worry out of report cards: we read (or paraphrase) them to our students before we send them home. Our principal has been creative in finding ways to free the teachers so they can have 10 to 15 minutes with each student for this purpose. We learn a lot about our students during this time. They have a chance to respond to what we've said, and we have an opportunity to explain why we said what we did, and what we meant. They love knowing what's on the report before it goes home. It relieves a lot of tension, and it helps them explain some of the comments to their parents.

It's important, for both the students and their parents, that the principal read and make a short comment on every report card. Those comments indicate that other people in the school, not just the classroom teacher, know and care about the children.

The Report Card Envelope

Another way to help students, especially younger ones, feel good about taking their report cards home is to give them a chance to decorate the envelope and make it special.

In the envelope might be any or all of the following:

- a note to the parents telling them what they should do with the other papers enclosed in the envelope (what to keep, what to sign, what to return);
- a letter describing the activities, trips and curriculum areas emphasized during the term (I believe, with many of my colleagues, that this item isn't necessary; the report should be complete enough to stand on its own — the letter doesn't usually stay with the report card anyway, and parents don't want to read pages of detailed program descriptions);
- the teacher's anecdotal report card;
- the student's own report card, either completed or ready to be filled in at home with a parent;
- samples of the student's writing or other work, chosen by the student (perhaps one from the beginning of the term and one more recent);
- a form for the parents' comments;
- an invitation to make an appointment for a parent-teacher interview, or an explanation of the upcoming student-led interview.

Summary

Encouraging report cards and helpful conferences sustain good communication and a positive spirit of cooperation. Our students' learning, attitudes and school experiences are the best they can be when children, teacher and parents support one another and work as a team.

REFERENCES

Forester, Anne D. and Margaret Reinhard. *The Learners' Way*. Winnipeg: Peguis Publishers, 1989.

Goodman, Yetta and Carolyn Burke. *Reading Miscue Inventory*. New York: Macmillan, 1972.

Little, Nancy and John Allen. *Student-led Teacher Parent Conferences*. Toronto: Lugus Publications, 1988.

Preece, Alison and Terry Johnson. "The Negotiated Report," in *Prime Areas*, Vol. 32, No. 3, Spring 1990.

SAMPLE FORMS

Subject:

Date:

Students:

Subject: _____ Date: _____

Students: _____

Subject: Date:

Students in Groups:	

Students:

My Lilypad Report

Most Favorite/Least Favorite — Color the numbers

Student: Date:

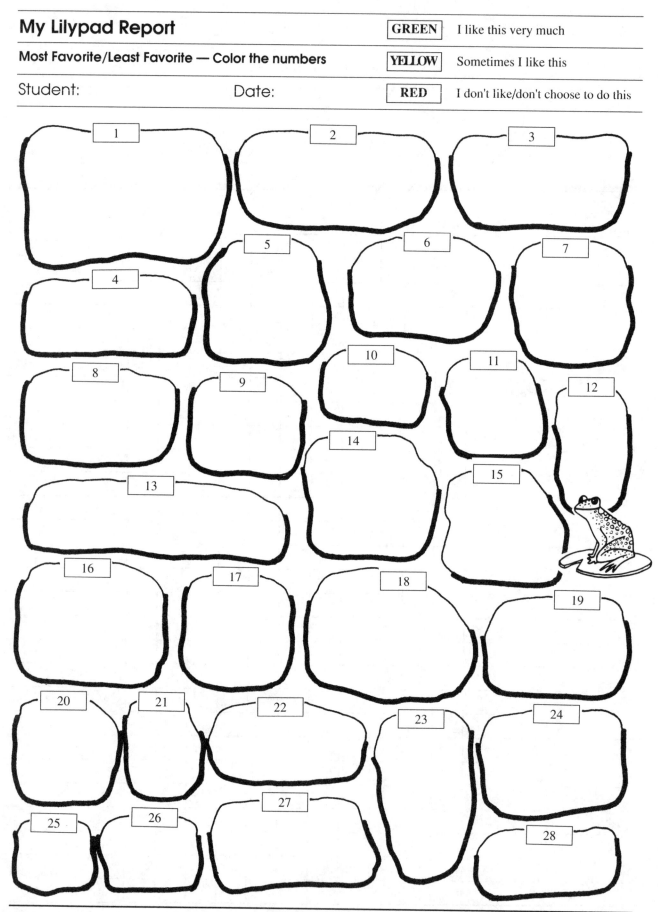

My Own Report Card

Date:

My Name:

My Age: years   months

My Teacher's Name:

**Social Skills
and
Work Habits**

◯ almost always   △ sometimes   ☁ no, not yet   ▢ no, not really

1. I listen to directions. .... ————

2. I follow directions. .... ————

3. I can work without bothering others. .... ————

4. I wait my turn to speak. .... ————

5. I listen to others when they speak. .... ————

6. I work well with others. .... ————

7. I am kind to others. .... ————

almost always   sometimes   no, not yet   no, not really

8. I keep my own things in order. .... _____

9. I clean up my own projects. .... _____

10. I help keep the classroom tidy. .... _____

11. I can solve disputes with other children
    without hurting them or fighting. .... _____

12. I follow school rules. .... _____

13. I enjoy recess. .... _____

Reading

	almost always	sometimes	no, not yet	no, not really

1. I enjoy looking at books. .... ———

2. I like to read. .... ———

3. I like to read at home. .... ———

4. I can often read new words without help. .... ———

5. I like to read Big Books with the class. .... ———

6. I enjoy partner reading. .... ———

7. I like to read to the whole class. .... ———

8. I like "quiet reading time" at school. .... ———

Writing

almost always ◯ sometimes △ no, not yet ☁ no, not really ▢

1. I like to write my own stories or poems. .... _____

2. Most of the time I can read what I have written. .... _____

3. I use upper case letters where they are needed. .... _____

4. I remember to use periods at the end of sentences. .... _____

5. I can print neatly. .... _____

6. I leave spaces between my words. .... _____

7. I enjoy using invented spelling. .... _____

8. I often spell words correctly in my own writing. .... _____

9. I participate well when we write together as a class. .... _____

○	△	⌇	□
almost always	sometimes	no, not yet	no, not really

Listening, Speaking, Drama

1. I like to speak in front of the class. .... ———

2. I feel at ease speaking to a small group. .... ———

3. I like to be in skits or plays. .... ———

4. I listen to other children when they are speaking to the group. ..... ———

5. I contribute to class discussions. .... ———

6. I like to listen to stories read out loud. .... ———

Mathematics

almost always   sometimes   no, not yet   no, not really

1. I like to work and play with numbers. .... ————

2. I can solve story problems. .... ————

3. I understand new ideas easily. .... ————

4. I understand math better when I use manipulative material. .... ————

Science

1. I like to learn new things about the world around me. .... ————

2. I like to watch and do experiments. .... ————

48

Social Studies

	almost always	sometimes	no, not yet	no, not really
○	△	☁	□

1. I am interested in learning about people and places. .... _____

2. I can work well with others in a group. .... _____

P.E.

1. I enjoy physical activies. .... _____

2. What I like to do best:
   A.   In the gym

   B.   Outside

Music

1. I like to sing with the class. .... _____

2. I like to learn about music. .... _____

Art

almost always · sometimes · no, not yet · no, not really

1. I like to draw ———— paint ————

   construct things ———— "cut and paste" ————

Other

1. I like to learn to speak and understand French. .... ————

2. I enjoy using the computer. .... ————

Buddy Time

With my "Big Buddy" I like to:

Activity Time

When I have the choice, these are the things I usually do: ....

My Own Anecdotal Report Card

Reading

Writing

Arithmetic

Music

Art

Behavior

Favorite Activities

Student: **Writing Self-Evaluation**

○ △ ☁
Yes   sometimes   not yet

In the writing I am evaluating ...

1. I wrote _____ sentences.

2. my spelling was   ❑   mostly invented

   ❑   mostly standard

   ❑   a mixture of both

3. I began my sentences with
   upper case letters. .... _____

4. I used periods or other punctuation
   in my sentences. .... _____

5. I separated my words. .... _____

6. I printed neatly. .... _____

7. I wrote interesting sentences. .... _____

8. I enjoyed writing. .... _____

My Teacher's Report Card

Date:

Student reporter:

Teacher's name:

Observations by **Parents**

Date:

Student: Teacher: Parent:

Teachers are interested in how you see your child at *home*. Please take a minute to make notes about his or her social and academic development, interests, attitudes, strengths and special needs.
When you write, use phrases or brief comments.

Your child's interactions with other children or with siblings:

Your child's interests and activities at home:

Your child's previous or present experiences that you consider significant:

Your child's structured activities outside school (sports, music, art lessons...?):

Observations by **Parents**

Date:

Student: Teacher: Parent:

Your child's attitude towards school and/or learning:

Your child's behavior:

Your child's special needs (environment, rules, learning style ...):

Your child's physical development:

Anything else?

Thank You   **Parent Signature:**

Parent-Teacher Conference

Student: Date:

Follow-up by **Parent**   Follow-up by **Teacher**